HOW TO GET RICH

How the average person can become wealthy

by
John L. Bowman

ISBN 978-0-578-50349-3

I dedicate this book to average
hard-working Americans.
May they get rich.

The cover is an image of a money tree superimposed on an American coin. Algamish said wealth is like a tree that grows from a tiny seed; the sooner you plant the seed, the sooner the tree shall grow.

Preface

There are a few things you should know about this book. It assumes you did not inherit wealth, you have little or no money, you never won the lottery, you know little about sources of wealth like the stock market and you did not have the business sense and good luck of Bill Gates. It assumes you are reasonably intelligent and have some degree of willpower.

This book assumes you live in a largely capitalistic and free market economy like America. It is in these political systems an individual can get rich. Highly socialistic and communistic societies discourage wealth accumulation, so I suspect the only avenue to wealth in these systems is the black market.

I am not a lawyer, tax expert or stock investment advisor. My views come from readings, experience in business and investing. You should always seek competent advice.

Most of the sources for this book are described in the acknowledgements. They are referred to often but not cited in endnotes. Rather, sources are usually credited in the text. Some sources are quoted verbatim, sometimes in quotation marks and sometimes in italics for emphasis, and some are paraphrased.

Finally, some of the sources for this book may not be accurate. George S. Clason's book *The Richest Man in Babylon*, for example, may not be historically true, but it makes a good story, so I assume it is.

Acknowledgements

I would like to acknowledge the following sources for this book. I based much of this book on George S. Clason's *The Richest Man in Babylon*. It is an inspiring book described in chapter two and referenced throughout this book. In chapter three, I used Michael Farr and Laurence Shatkin's *300 Best Jobs Without a Four-Year Degree* (in which most information came from the United States Department of Labor). I also used Frank Bettger's timeless book on selling, *How I Raised Myself from Failure to Success in Selling*.

In chapter four I relied on *The Forbes Stock Market Course*, which is an indispensable source of basic information on stocks. In chapters four and five on stocks, I relied heavily on Benjamin Graham's *The Intelligent Investor* and Peter L. Lynch's *Beating the Street*. These are two of the best books available on investing in stocks. I also used *Rich Dad, Poor Dad* by Robert Kiyosaki, whose wise advice is sprinkled throughout the book.

For chapter six, I used various sources including the National Association of Realtors, my family budget, my business and my Hewlett Packard 12C calculator.

In chapter seven, I used Judith Wallenstein, Julia Lewis and Sandra Blakeslee's insightful book *The Unexpected Legacy of Divorce.* In chapters one and nine. I used James Buchanan's *Frozen Desire*, which is a wonderful book about the nature of money, and in chapter nine, I referenced M. M. Kirsch's book *How to Get Off the Fast Track and Live a Life Money Can't Buy.*

I would like to thank the following contributors to this book: Marlene McCartney of H&R Block in Portland, Oregon reviewed the Save section in chapter six and Taxes in chapter seven. Gene Bentley, CCIM and former commissioner of the Oregon Real Estate Agency, reviewed my calculations in chapter six on savings and mortgage prepayment and house appreciation in chapter seven on inflation. I would also like to thank my wife Kathy for her many good suggestions and Kathryn Banks for editing and formatting the book.

Finally, please excuse me, but I also used many of my own books including *A Reference Guide to Stoicism, Philosophy and Happiness*, *Stoicism, Enkrasia and Happiness* and *Provocative and Contemplative Quotations.* Many of my thoughts and information came from my life experiences, general knowledge and Google. I endeavored to cite all of these sources in the text of this manuscript.

Contents

II Things that Enhance Wealth Accumulation

    Save
    Buy a House
    Budget
    Own a Business
    Carry Insurance

III Things that Detract from Wealth Accumulation

        Inflation
        Debt
        Taxes
        Divorce

IV The Big Picture

Introduction

This book is about how the average person can get rich. It is written for those with a modest income, without wealth or a college degree. This is not a book about how to get rich quick. It is about how to live life and think in certain ways that bring wealth. If you can do what this book says, I believe you will get rich.

The book will methodically take you through steps to get rich. It first asks if you have the character, and if you don't, it suggests saving yourself from disappointment by doing something else. The ability to get rich has much to do with your character and how you think.

George Clason's book *The Richest Man in Babylon* begins your quest for gold because it outlines the fundamental requirements to achieve wealth. Many cannot get rich because they have low-paying jobs, so the next topic is how to get a good paying job without a college. Many may find chapters four and five on stocks dull, but they are important because this is how you will get rich. Chapter four is about stocks, and chapter five discusses which stocks to invest in.

The book then explains things that enhance and distract from wealth accumulation. Saving, buying a house, budgeting, owning a business and carrying insurance enhance it, and inflation, debt, taxes and divorce hinder it. Throughout this book, twenty-seven rules of how to get rich are developed, which are summarized in chapter eight.

The beginning of the book asks if you have the character to get rich, and the last chapter, which is my favorite, asks you if will be happy if you do get rich. It is about the philosophic big picture and the interesting relationship between money and happiness.

I hope my book helps you, and I hope you get rich.

I

The Plan to Accumulate Wealth

Chapter One
Character

There are two questions you need to ask yourself before you embark on getting rich. The first is whether you have the character to do so, the topic of this chapter, and the second is if you will be happy if you achieve wealth, which is the topic of the last chapter.

For most people, getting rich is not easy — it takes considerable time and effort. So, you should have a serious conversation with yourself to see if you have the ability to get rich. It should be an honest self-evaluation of your personality. John Locke wrote in *An Essay Concerning Human Understanding* that "'tis of great use to the sailor to know the length of his line"; you need to know the length of your line, or strengths and weakness, in order to make an objective view of yourself — if you cheat you are only cheating yourself.

There are eight characteristics that succor wealth creation. The first is the ability to reason. You need to be able to organize and direct yourself and understand the consequences of causes. Reason, for example, tells you that you need to budget and follow through with an investment program; what benefits you will gain by these actions. Reason also helps you control the second required characteristic — the ability to control your passions and in particular desire. James Buchanan in his book *Frozen Desire* wrote that "the world is a battlefield of limitless, unsatisfied wishes and desires which money makes conspicuous" and that money makes concrete sensations like the sensation of wanting like a clock does the sensation of time. Everyone is burdened by more desires than they can gratify, so you must be able to give up wanting more.

The third characteristic is industriousness. Getting rich requires hard work — indolence gets you nothing. Are you a hard-working person? The fourth characteristic is courage. To get rich you need the courage to try something new like getting a higher paying job or pursuing an investment program and to take the natural risks that accompany the accumulation of wealth — you must be able to act. If you are faint of heart and believe the sky is falling when the Dow Jones Industrial Average tanks, wealth may not be for you.

The fifth characteristic is the ability to be self-directed, self-disciplined, single-minded and focused. You need to be able to consistently do what it takes to get rich. Capricious people rarely get rich. The sixth characteristic is to have the right attitude. A positive outlook sees setbacks as temporary, whereas a negative one sees them as insurmountable obstacles. There will be many setbacks in your pursuit of wealth that you must overcome with a positive attitude.

The seventh characteristic is perseverance. When you face a problem, do you give up or redouble your efforts to solve it? You must be able to weather the ups and downs in life and the stock market. You need a steadiness of conviction and the ability to finish what you start. The final characteristic is patience. It takes time to accumulate wealth, which requires a quiet willingness to wait for the ultimate reward. You need to be able to take the long view in life.

If you decide you do not have these characteristics, you can save yourself a lot of pain. It may be that you will be far happier seeking the security of being a banker or government worker or more fulfilled being an artist. If you think you do have these characteristics, however, follow the advice in this book and the odds are you will get rich.

Whether you decide you have the characteristics to get rich or not, one constant remains, which is that it is in your interests to pay attention to money. Those who say they are not interested in money are in denial because they work for it all day. Indeed, those who are concerned with money early in life are the ones who think about it the least late in life, whereas those that feigned unconcern with money early in life think about it all the time later because they have none.

This brings us to the First Rule of How to Get Rich—decide if you have the character to get rich. If you do, let's move on and learn how to get rich.

Chapter Two
The Richest Man in Babylon

George S. Clason wrote a profound little book titled *The Richest Man in Babylon* that is about how to get rich. Its central character is a certain Arkad, the richest man in Babylon who explained the rules of gold. Some, like Clason, believe the ancient city of Babylon existed eight thousand years ago, while others claim it arose later, but in either case, it is a very old city. It is known, for example, that the ancient historian Herodotus visited Babylon probably in the fifth century BCE. In any case, Arkad's rules were preserved on clay tablets that were unearthed by archeologists.

Arkad's clay tablets described various cures for a lean purse such as getting a good job, budgeting, investing, insurance and buying a home as well as some rules for gold, which included saving and getting good advice. This chapter will describe Arkad's rules in detail, which rules will be expanded on in later chapters.

Arkad's rules of gold ascribed to him by George Clason are timeless ways to accumulate wealth. These rules are as true today as they were millennia ago in ancient Babylon. Like the Arkads of the ages, learn and obey these rules and you too will get rich.

The Men Who Desired Gold

Clason's book begins with a conversation between two friends, Bansir and Kobbi. Bansir is a chariot builder and Kobbi a musician, and both, after half a lifetime of hard labor, lament that they have empty purses. Bansir says that he is wearied of working, working, working and going nowhere. He says that he does not want to go on year after year living a slavish, poor life. He says he wants to be a man of means. Kobbi, who is of the same mind, agrees and suggests they try and find out how to acquire gold. He suggests they go see their friend Arkad, the richest man in Babylon, to learn how to get rich. Unwittingly, Bansir and Kobbi discovered the second rule of gold; their purses were empty because they never decided to pursue it. Most people only dream of acquiring wealth but never do anything about it. This gives us the Second Rule of How to Get Rich—make the decision to become rich and do what it takes to acquire wealth.

The Richest Man in Babylon

So, Bansir and Kobbi went to see Arkad. Arkad, a thoughtful man interested in others, was happy to help his young friends. He explained that he had learned the rules of gold when he was young from the money lender Algamish. Algamish told him there are four things you need to know. First, understand that part of all you earn is yours to keep, so save one-tenth of everything you earn. Second, live on less than you earn. Third, make your gold work for you, and fourth, seek advice from competent men. Algamish finished by telling Arkad that wealth is like a tree that grows from a tiny seed, and the sooner you plant the seed, the sooner the tree shall grow. Arkad said he thanked Algamish, and then he wished Bansir and Kobbi good luck.

Seven Cures for a Lean Purse

The king of Babylon, who knew Arkad was his wealthiest citizen, wanted all Babylonians to learn the cures for a lean purse, so he asked Arkad if he would teach everyone the rules of gold, which Arkad said he would be pleased to do. Arkad pondered what to say, decided to expand on Algamish's advice with some of his own experience and gave a speech to the citizens of Babylon that summarized the timeless seven cures for a lean purse.

The first rule was to start your purse to fattening by keeping 10 percent of all you earn. He said for every ten coins thou placest within thy purse, take out for use but nine. Hence the Third Rule of How to Get Rich—save 10 percent of all you earn. I will expand on this simple principle in chapter six with dollar-cost averaging. The second rule was to control thy expenditures. Arkad explained that all men are burdened with more desires than they can gratify unless they protest to the contrary. Arkad explained the solution was to budget thy expenses that thou mayest have coins to pay for thy necessities, to pay for thy enjoyments and to gratify thy worthwhile desires without spending more than nine-tenths of thy earnings. In today's terms, this means to live within your means and spend less than you make. This leads to the Fourth Rule of How to Get Rich—control your expenditures through budgeting—and the Fifth Rule of How to Get Rich—spend less than you make.

Arkad's third point was to make thy gold multiply. He told them to put each coin to laboring so it may reproduce its kind as the flocks of the field and help bring to thee income, a stream of wealth that shall flow constantly into thy purse. In other words, invest your savings, which gives the Sixth Rule of How to Get Rich—invest and make your gold multiply. This will be expanded in chapter five on investing.

Arkad next told them to guard thy treasures from loss, which was his fourth point. He said secure thy treasure from loss by investing only where thy principal is safe, where it may be reclaimed if desirable and where thou will not fail to collect a fair rental. This means two things: invest in a way that conserves your principle and carry insurance in case of loss. The first will be discussed in chapters four and five, and the second gives us the Seventh Rule of How to Get Rich—carry insurance, which will be discussed in chapter six. His fifth point was to make of thy dwelling a profitable investment. This both reduces your cost of living and brings an asset that will increase in value. Hence, the Eighth Rule of How to Get Rich—buy a house.

Arkad's sixth point was to insure a future income. He said you should provide in advance for the needs of thy growing age and protection of thy family. To achieve this, small payments with regularity doth produce profitable results. His seventh and final point was to increase thy ability to earn. He said the man who seeks to learn more of his craft shall be richly rewarded, so study your craft and become wiser and more skillful. This gives us the Ninth Rule of How to Get Rich—get a good job and get better at it.

The Five Rules of Gold

The King of Babylon was so impressed with Arkad's seven cures for a lean purse he had them condensed and engraved on clay tablets. This is what the archeologists found thousands of years later, which summarized the five rules of gold. The first rule is:

> Gold cometh to any man who will put away
> one-tenth of his earnings. Gold cometh glad-
> ly and in increasing quantity to any man

who will put by not less than one-tenth of his earnings to create an estate for his future and that of his family.

Save part of your income on a regular basis. The second rule is:

Gold laboreth for the wise owner who finds for it profitable employment. Gold laboreth diligently and contentedly for the wise owner who finds for its profitable employment, multiplying even as the flocks in the field.

Wisely invest your savings and make them multiply. The third rule is:

Gold clingeth to those who invest it under the advice of wise men. Gold clingeth to the protection of the cautious owner who invests it under the advice of men wise in its handling.

When investing your savings listen to the advice of wise men. One contemporary wise man, Benjamin Graham wrote in The Intelligent Investor that investing money in securities is unique because it almost always is based on advice from others, which advice should be conservative. He cautioned that an elementary requirement for the intelligent investor is the ability to resist the blandishments of salesman offering new common-stock issues during bull markets. This brings us to the Tenth Rule of How to

14

Get Rich — listen to the advice of wise men.
   The fourth rule is:

> Gold slippeth away from men who invest in
> businesses with which they are not familiar.
> Gold slippeth away from the man who in-
> vests it in businesses or purposes with which
> he is not familiar or which are not approved
> by those skilled in its keep.

Invest only in that which you know or with those who
do know. This gives us the Eleventh Rule of How to Get
Rich — invest in what you or trusted others know.
   The fifth and final rule is:

> Gold flees the man who would force it to
> impossible earnings who followeth the allur-
> ing advice of tricksters and schemers or who
> trusts it to his own inexperience and roman-
> tic desires in investment.

First, do not seek exorbitant speculative returns. Do
not be swayed by the fantastic plans of impractical men
who offer ways to force thy gold to make earnings un-
usually large. Such plans are the creations of dreamers
unskilled in the safe and dependable laws of trade. It is
better to have a little caution than a great regret. Second,
do not trust inexperienced and untested advisors. Graham, quoting an old French proverb, wrote that bright,
energetic people, usually young, have promised to perform miracles with other people's money since time im-

memorial. They have usually been able to do it for a while but inevitably brought losses to their public in the end. So, associate with men and enterprises that have established their ability to invest wisely and be protected by their wisdom and experience. Finally, do not invest in what you do not know or for non-financial reasons. Robert Kiyosaki in *Rich Dad, Poor Dad* put it this way: learn to distinguish between those who speak from emotion and those who speak from clear thought. This brings us to the Twelfth Rule of How to Get Rich — don't speculate with your savings.

The seven cures for a lean purse and five rules of gold are the timeless ways to accumulate wealth. They work as well today as they did thousands of years ago for the richest man in Babylon. Follow these simple rules, and you will acquire wealth.

Meet the Goddess of Good Luck

George Clason had one last piece of advice from antiquity. He wrote that men of action are favored by the goddess of good luck, which in contemporary terms means fortune favors the brave. Fortune favors the brave because the bold see more opportunities; by seeking what they want, they recognize opportunities when they appear. Niccolò Machiavelli in *The Prince* once wrote that it is better to be impetuous than cautious, for fortune is a woman, and it is necessary, if you wish to master her, to conquer her by force; and it can be seen that she lets herself be overcome by the bold rather than by those who proceed coldly. In your life, job and investing be prudential but also courageous and bold in action. This gives us the Thirteenth Rule of How to Get Rich — be a person of action.

If you are a contemporary Bansir or Kobbi, listen to Arkad's advice and get rich. Save part of what you earn, live within your means, invest your savings, avoid risky investments, invest only to make money, listen to the advice of wise men and be bold.

I would add three unwritten suggestions to Arkad's advice. First, be a problem solver. The rich man looks at life as a series of problems to be solved and solves them, such as the problem of how to get rich. The poor men only whine and complain. Second, work hard. Work is your friend because it keeps you from Voltaire's three great evils, which are vice, boredom and poverty. Being industrious is a prerequisite to becoming rich. Finally, be persistent. Quitters rarely get rich, whereas those with determination will prevail in time. Those with determination usually find a way to succeed. This gives us the Fourteenth Rule of How to Get Rich — never give up.

So let us move on and find out how to get a good paying job in the next chapter.

Chapter Three
Get a Good Job and Get Better at It

It is difficult to save, invest and get rich if you do not have a decent income. George Clason earlier wrote about the need to increase your ability to earn. So, this chapter addresses how the average person without a four-year college degree can get a high paying job. The formula is simple: pick the right job, get better at it and practice salesmanship.

The United States Department of Labor listed some of the highest and lowest paying jobs in America. Some of the highest predictably include chief executives, lawyers and physicians but also computer and information systems managers, software developers, purchasing managers, personal financial advisors and marketing and sales managers. Some of the lowest paying jobs also predictably include hairdresser, retail salesperson, bartender, butcher, food server, laborer, janitor, hotel and motel clerk, cook and agricultural worker.

There are four things to keep in mind when picking the right job in life. The first is rather obvious, choose a high paying job and avoid the low paying ones. Second, it is fine if you are hell-bent on working at a low paying job, but be aware that your odds of getting rich are low. For example, if you have a burning desire to be a hairdresser, know that the Bureau of Labor Statistics shows that hair-stylists make a median wage of $24,950 a year. This is not enough to get rich. It is rewarding to work at what interests you, but if you want to get rich, it is more rewarding to pick a high paying job that interests you.

The third point is that not all high paying jobs require a four-year college degree. Certainly, it is best to get a four-year college degree. It not only makes your life richer but also increases pay. Various recent studies from Georgetown University and the Pew Research Center indicate that over their lifetimes, college graduates on average earn $1 million more than non-college graduates and that the yearly income gap between high school and college graduates is around $17,500.

The book *300 Best Jobs Without a Four-Year Degree* by Michael Farr and Laurence Shatkin, PhD, has a section titled *The 100 Best-Paying Jobs that Don't Require a Four-Year Degree*. Some of those jobs (along with their annual earnings) include air-traffic controller ($102,030), storage and distribution manger ($66,600), real estate broker ($58,720), medical sales manager ($58,350), freight inspector ($50,380) and subway and streetcar operator ($49,290). Some of these skills can be learned on the job, as an apprentice or from a technical or trade school. So if you don't have a four-year college degree take heart—find a high paying job that does not require one and learn it.

The fourth point is that most high paying jobs involve the brain rather than brawn. Most of the high paying jobs listed earlier in the United States Department of Labor's highest paying jobs involved the brain. It is better to work at a job with your brain than brawn. So pick the job that interests you that uses your brain.

However, this is not always the case. It is harder, but you can get rich with your brawn also. For example, the Bureau of Labor Statistics show that an automotive service technician's (aka auto mechanic) 2017 median annual wage was $39,550; however, the top 10 percent earned $65,430. So you can learn to be an auto mechanic, get better at your job and earn up to $65,000 a year. You can get rich on this.

How do you learn how to do your high paying job that does not require a four-year college degree? There is a virtual plethora of options. Some mentioned earlier include learn on the job, learn at a business, be an apprentice or go to a technical or trade school. Others include vocational schools and community colleges. *Forbes* magazine listed some of the top two-year trade schools in America, which include North Central Kansas Technical College, State Technical College of Missouri, Lake Area Technical Institute, Lancaster County Career and Technology Center and the Mitchell Technical Institute. See what is available where you live.

Of course, the next question is how much it will cost and how you can pay for it. The College Resource Network wrote that some of the tuitions of two-year community, trade and technical schools range from $4,413 to $17,000 per year. Beg or borrow the money to attend these schools because it is a good investment. If you need to borrow, the College Resource Network also wrote that virtually all tuitions are covered by financial aid of some kind. It is also encouraging to note that many of the schools had 100 percent acceptance rates.

So, there is your path to a high paying job. Get a four-year college degree or get a technical/vocational education. But that is not enough. Now you need to get better at your job. The auto mechanics that make $65,000 a year improved their skills. To make the most money in your trade, you must get better at it—you need to know how to do your job better than anyone else. You need to become valuable and sought after—you need to gain a reputation as the best at what you do.

The ancient Greeks had a word for this, which is arête. It means virtue or loosely to be the best of your kind—to be the best that you can be. You should have arête in your job. It is none of my business, but if you want to live a successful life, you should have arête in all aspects of your life such as in parenting, marriage and citizenship—but that is another book. Remember the Ninth Rule of How to Get Rich in the last chapter—get a good job and get better at it.

Not mentioned in this chapter is how you can get rich by owning a business. Doing so is one significant way to get rich without a four-year college degree. This will be discussed in chapter six.

I will finish this chapter by discussing two authors whose advice is worth heeding in your job—Benjamin Franklin and Frank Bettger. Franklin's thirteen virtues included *lose not time* (be industrious and focus on your job), *always be employed in something useful* (endeavor to advance in your job), *cut off all unnecessary actions* (be efficient at your job), *resolve to perform as you ought* (always do a good job) and *be honest* (if you are square with the world you will never go wrong). This gives us the Fifteenth Rule of How to Get Rich—be virtuous.

Lesser known Bettger wrote an important book titled *How I Raised Myself from Failure to Success in Selling* in which he described how to be a good salesperson. Bettger was failing at his sales job, so he studied how to become a better salesman and succeeded. Although most of his advice is for people in sales, much of it applies to all jobs and life in general. The truth is that the most successful people in life are those who know salesmanship. It is a way to learn about and help others in order to distinguish yourself and succeed. It is about how to be successful by being other-regarding. Like it or not, the most successful doctors and lawyers are good salespeople.

I will mention fourteen of his points here because they relate to your job. His first and perhaps most important point is to find out what people want and then help them get it. Think in terms of others' wants, desires and needs. This is easier said than done because people often camouflage their needs, so to find them he suggests always asking "why, and in addition to that…" in order to get the person talking. The successful doctor not only cures but also addresses fears and inspires trust, and the best auto mechanic not only repairs cars but also gives his clients advice on what they can do to keep their cars running better and longer. In both cases, they gained lifelong patients and clients.

Other points include the need to have enthusiasm, to be prepared, to ask questions, to express appreciation for your listener's ability, to be a good listener, to gain confidence by being bluntly honest, to look your best, to make understatements (and never exaggerate), to remember people's names, to be brief and to the point and to never fear failure (failure is nothing if success comes eventually). One point mentioned earlier is to know your business and keep learning your business (the Ninth Rule of How to Get Rich was get a good job and get better at it). The final point is to always be punctual (one successful businessman once said *he who steals my time steals my money*). These points give us our Sixteenth Rule of How to Get Rich — learn salesmanship.

Get a good job, get better at it and start your purse a-fattening. The next chapter is about learning how to invest your purse so it continues to fatten.

Chapter Four
Learn about Stocks

So you have decided that you have the character to get rich and decided to do so. You then, like Bansir and Kobbi, learned the simple rules of gold's acquisition. Then you got a good paying job and got better at it, so you have some savings. Now how do you invest your savings to get rich? You do so by learning about stocks, the topic of this chapter, and investing your savings in stocks, which is the topic of the next chapter. Benjamin Graham in *The Intelligent Investor* wrote that there is a great advantage for the young capitalist to begin his financial education—and this early education should include stocks.

So, let's get started. First, I don't expect you to become a stock expert. Most of your investments in stocks will be made with the help of an investment advisor, sometimes called an account executive and historically a stock broker. How to pick one will be discussed in the next chapter. The reason to learn something about stocks is so you can tell your future advisor what you want and have the ability to recognize poor advice — you should know enough about stocks to be dangerous (not so much because you should be, but rather so you can recognize if your stock advisor is). Second, this book's subtitle is *how the average person can become wealthy*, so I will assume you have some knowledge about money but not stocks.

Let's begin with the definitions of a few simple basic stock terms you should know.

> • Bear market: A market in which prices are falling thus encouraging selling
> • Blue-chip stocks: Shares of very large, well organized companies with a long history of sound financial performance
> • Bull market: A market in which share prices are rising thus encouraging buying
> • Common stock: Securities that represent an ownership in a corporation
> • Dividend: An amount paid to stockholders
> • Dow Jones Industrial Average (DOW): A leading stock index that measures the average prices of industrial, transportation and utility stocks (two other significant exchange indexes are the

National Association of Securities Dealers Auto-mated Quotations [NASDAQ] and Standard and Poor's 500 [S&P 500])

• New York Stock Exchange (NYSE): A stock ex-change located in New York City that is consid-ered the largest equities-based exchange in the world

• Odd lot: An amount of stocks other than the stan-dard trading unit of one hundred (the ownership of sixty-nine stocks is an odd lot)

• Preferred stock: A stock whose dividend must be paid before any dividend for common stock

• Price-earnings (p/e) ratio: The current market price of a company share divided by the earnings per share of the company (the higher the p/e ratio, the more speculative the stock)

• Return: The gain or loss on an investment ex-pressed as a percentage of the investments cost, or in plain terms, how much you make on your investment

• Round lot: An amount of stocks equal to one hun-dred (ownership of one hundred shares of stocks is a round lot)

• Securities and Exchange Commission (SEC): A federal agency that administers various federal laws and regulates the securities industry

• Securities Protection Insurance Corporation (SPIC): This provides some coverage to investors if their brokerage firm becomes insolvent

• Stock mutual fund: A portfolio of stocks made up of many different diversified assets

• Stock split: Increasing the number of shares of a corporation by granting existing shareholders more shares. If you own one hundred shares in a corporation and it declares a two-for-one split, you end up owning two hundred shares

• Ticker symbol: An abbreviation used to identify publicly traded shares of a particular company's stock (for example, 3M Company's ticker symbol on the New York Stock Exchange is MMM)

• Yield: The amount you receive annually in dividends or interest on your stock divided by the amount you spent on the stock

It would be reasonable to ask here why you should use stocks to become wealthy rather than other investments. So, let's look at a few of the reasons. You could get wealthy by inheriting money, but if you, like most people, have no wealthy ancestors, you are out of luck. You could try and marry a rich person but they are rare and probably already married, and you would most likely get a divorce because you married for the wrong reason. You could try to get rich gambling or winning the lottery, but the odds are so low that you most likely would remain poor. Some like to invest in gold or diamonds, but they pay no dividends, are often speculative and generally have low returns. Many invest in commodities, but they are also risky and you may lose your savings.

Some more conventional vehicles to wealth include bank certificates of deposit, bonds and treasury bills. These are safe ways to accumulate capital but they usually have low returns, do not appreciate and can sometimes decline in value. Bonds, for example, go down in value if interest rates increase and inflation often erodes their gains.

Three promising possibilities include your job, investing in real estate and starting a business. These are often reliable ways to wealth that are mentioned in this book. Getting a good job with a high salary can bring wealth, but it is impeded by taxation and is not always sustainable. Investing in real estate is a reliable way to wealth but it requires considerable knowledge, involves risk and debt and is not liquid. Starting your own business is another way to wealth, but it is fraught with challenges including your business acumen, the initial debt, changing markets and overhead, along with a host of other problems.

Stocks are historically the most reliable way to become wealthy — they are profitable. Peter Lynch in *Beating the Street* wrote that over the last seventy years stocks have gained 11 percent per year due to 3 percent dividend and 8 percent appreciation compared to treasury bonds and certificates of deposit whose returns have been half that. Graham wrote that stocks have paid a higher average return to investors over the years, which offers considerable protection against the erosion of your money caused by inflation.

Robert Kiyosaki in *Rich Dad, Poor Dad* made the important point that to get rich you need to accumulate assets that pay you when you are not working. Unlike your job, stocks are assets that do just that — they pay dividends whether you work or not. They also often appreciate in value, are less risky, are liquid and require no upfront debt to acquire if you pay cash. Further, if you accumulate stocks in a tax-deferred program like an individual retirement account (IRA), the income your stocks compound over the years is tax-deferred. Acquiring stocks is a time-tested formula for getting wealthy.

So if you decide your wealth is to be in stocks, you should learn more about them. The *Forbes Stock Market Course* is an excellent source of basic knowledge about stocks and is a good place to begin.

To fully understand which individual stocks to purchase, *Forbes* suggests you study a newspaper's financial page. You should notice a stock's fifty-two week high and low, its annual dividend rate, its yield, its price-earnings ratio, its range or high and low price of the day, its closing price, the net price change from its previous close and the daily volume traded.

Forbes also suggests you know market trends and then gives some advice on them. They suggest watching the breadth of the market (the number of stocks traded, stocks advancing and stocks declining) and the volume of trading, which they consider one of the most significant trends because it shows the quality and quantity of buying and selling, and keeping track of the Dow Jones stock average. Some of their advice includes the importance of focusing on the underlying strength of the economy and businesses, that business failures give advance warning of a stock market decline, that stock prices tend to run ahead of the course of business activity, that when business for heavy backbone companies like steel and auto slow it means the market is heading into lean times and when their business is good it heralds a rising trend, and

30

that trends never last indefinitely — they come to turning points.

Much of *Forbes*'s specific advice on the stock market deals with bull and bear markets. Few like bear markets because their wealth declines. Declining market tops herald the beginning of a bear market. This is when the DOW hits a certain high point, recedes from it but never again reaches it again, even on rallies. Bear markets usually begin violently and end quietly and are always followed by a rise in prices. The time to buy stocks is at the end of a bear market. Generally, bear markets follow four phases: the initial sharp break, a period of heavy liquidation, a series of intermediate rallies followed by declines and then a prolonged period of dullness. Everybody likes bull markets because their wealth increases. The good news is that bull markets usually last twice as long as bear markets — usually seven years.

Generally, *Forbes* explains that bear markets start violently, whereas bull markets start very gradually, almost imperceptibly, that it is easier to identify the start of a new bull market than the start of a new bear market and that most money is lost at the end of a bull market and the beginning of a bear market. In either case take heart because bull and bear markets follow each other as surely as night follows day — the bull will become a bear and the bear a bull.

Forbes concludes on stock markets with a few wisdoms from Wall Street that are worth remembering. Never enter a hopeless situation, patience pays, always have some cash available for bargains so you can buy when others are selling, caution is the father of security, cut your losses short, let your profits run, diversify your holdings and keep in mind that the market will always do what it should do (but not always when it should).

The best way to invest in stocks is through dollar-cost averaging. *Forbes* describes this method as the best for the conservative investor with a minimum of time to study stocks, a painless way to accumulate a capital fund and a way to eliminate the problem of timing stock purchases. They advise this approach because it is a systematic way of investing dividends that speeds up the compounding effect. This is good advice that will be expanded on in the next chapter.

Here I must give my reader a warning—there are no guarantees in life, and you may not get rich investing in the stock market. Peter Lynch wrote that over the past seventy years there have been forty scary declines of 10 percent or more in the stock market of which thirteen have been over 33 percent. In 1901 to 1903 the DOW declined 45.3 percent, in 1929 to 1932 it declined 89.2 percent and in 1973 to 1974 it declined 45.1 percent. It is probable you will get rich investing in stocks but not guaranteed.

So, you are thinking you have learned enough about stocks. Certainly, you have gained a degree of financial literacy and understand that wealth comes from owning part of a business through stocks. Indeed, *Forbes* explained when you purchase stock in a company you are actually purchasing a share of ownership in that company. You have also now learned the reason for the Seventeenth Rule of How to Get Rich—learn about stocks.

But this is not enough, you still need to know which stocks to own. So, the next chapter is about getting a financial advisor, determining which stocks to buy, comparing the advice of two stock rock stars, Benjamin Graham and Peter Lynch, learning more about dollar-cost averaging and finally deciding what vehicle to use to invest in stocks.

Chapter Five

Invest in Stocks

This chapter is about learning which stocks to own with Benjamin Graham and Peter Lynch, how to acquire them through dollar-cost averaging and how to own them through a tax-deferred retirement account. I know this can be boring, but hang in there because this is about your wealth.

First, you need to get a financial advisor. Recall Arkad's fifth rule of gold, which was to avoid the advice of tricksters and schemers, and the Tenth Rule of How to Get Rich, which was to listen to the advice of wise men. You need a wise stock investment advisor who is knowledgeable and trustworthy. Graham wrote that most advisors are individuals of good character, but it is easy to fall into incompetent and unscrupulous hands, so finding the right advisor is critical. Graham suggests selecting one from a brokerage firm with the highest reputation — a well-established and well-recommended investment counsel firm. He wrote to be wary of brokers who promise spectacular profits because speculating in stocks is "almost condemned by mathematical law to lose in the end." He also wrote that much bad advice is given free, so you should not take advice from relatives, friends or someone with a hot stock tip.

Graham also makes the point that you should tell your advisor that you are a value-minded investor and not quotation-minded so they know you are a serious investor. You should tell them that you want to invest in high-grade income stocks of leading corporations whose prices are not too high.

Two problems you will encounter at this point are first that the best advisors may not want you because you are a small account and second that you will have to pay your advisor a fee. On the first problem, perhaps you can find a less-established but knowledgeable and honest advisor who will pay attention to your portfolio rather than an experienced one who won't. On the second problem, if your advisor is a good one, the fee is worth it. Fees vary, but with an established, sizeable portfolio, 1 percent per year is common.

So, now let us get into which stocks to buy — a daunting task. *Forbes*, for example, says in a recession you should own companies not seriously affected by recessions like soft drinks, liquor and public utilities and avoid companies strongly affected by recessions like steel, rail equipment, machinery and luxury items like jewelry. In order to sort this out, I will offer some advice from two great stock advisors, the cautious, defensive, intellectual financial analyst Graham and the risk-taking, street-wise stock picker Lynch. I think this is an unbeatable combination; between the two lie the answers, so I will describe where they agree shortly.

In his book *The Intelligent Investor*, Graham emphasizes the need to be a defensive investor and to not panic when stocks decline. He wrote that the majority of security owners should elect to be defensive because they do not have the time, determination or mental equipment to be an aggressive investor. Much of his book is about human psychology. He wrote that it is virtually impossible to predict the price movements of stocks, so you should be prepared financially and psychologically for adverse results. He points out that a decline in the stock market does not mean you are losing money if you have not sold. Some specific advice from Graham is to buy larger companies who are going through a period of unpopularity, to buy bargain stocks or ones that are selling for one-half their value and to avoid high-priced blue-chip stocks.

Peter Lynch in *Beating the Street* wrote that if successful stocks could be picked by measurement, the mathematicians and accountants would all be rich—he believes it takes a knack or hunch to pick profitable stocks. Lynch says you should focus on stocks that have an unbroken twenty-year record of dividend increases. A Google search provided the names of twenty-five companies that have raised their dividends for the past twenty-five years or more. A few of these blue-chip stocks are (along with their ticker symbol) 3M Company (MMM), Coca-Cola Company (KO), Exxon Mobil (XOM), Johnson & Johnson (JBJ) and Kimberly-Clark Corporation (KMB). You can find the rest with a little work.

Risk-taking Lynch believes recessions are the holy grail of the stock picker—the latest correction is not a disaster but an opportunity to acquire more shares at low prices. You can pick up bargains left behind by investors who are fleeing the storm in panic. He believes this is how great fortunes are made. He eschews bull markets when everything is overpriced. Finally, he wrote that over the long haul, it is better to buy stocks in small companies.

Although Graham and Lynch differ somewhat in their stock philosophies, they have much in common. Following are eleven points of wisdom where they agree. First, they agree to buy quality stocks. Graham wrote that investing involves safety of principle and adequate return—everything else is speculative. Lynch wrote that you will be better off in the long run to own quality dividend-paying stocks. Second, buy prominent well-managed companies with a history of prosperity. Graham advised to select large, prominent and conservatively financed companies, and Lynch to buy stocks in well-managed growth companies with a history of prosperity and earnings on the rise.

Third, both emphasize that you should buy companies with a long record of dividend paying. For Graham, they should have an unbroken twenty-year record of dividend increases and for Lynch, they should usually increase their dividends yearly. Fourth, you should buy stock based on the company and not the stock. For Graham, look to the business and not the stock, and for Lynch, know the company before you buy the stock.

Other points of agreement include the need to diversify, the fifth point. Graham advises owning at least ten different issues. Their sixth point of agreement, which was mentioned earlier, is the importance of not panicking when stocks decline. Graham wrote that the investor who permits himself to be stampeded or unduly worried by unjustified market declines in his holdings is perversely transforming his basic advantage—the right not to sell— into a basic disadvantage. Lynch is particularly emphatic on this point. He wrote frankly that everyone has the brainpower to make money in stocks, but not everyone has the stomach. If you are susceptible to selling everything in a panic, you ought to avoid stocks. Be patient and do not sell a stock because the sky is falling.

Their seventh point is to focus on safety and not to speculate. Graham wrote that if you speculate you will probably lose and Lynch that long shots almost always miss the mark. You should focus on safety, simplicity of choice, the promise of satisfactory returns and containing your losses. Lynch believes there is no shame in losing money in a stock (everyone does it), but what is shameful is to hold on to a stock, or worse buy more of it, when the fundamentals are deteriorating. Their eighth point is to know what you are doing. Indeed, one of Lynch's Peter Principles is to never invest in any idea you can't illustrate with a crayon—you need to explain or understand what the company does; if you can't, don't buy it.

Their ninth point is to seek competence, which was discussed earlier. For Graham, do not let anyone else run your business unless they are competent, and for Lynch, ignore the herd. Their tenth point is invest for profit, which is echoed by Robert Kiyosaki in his book *Rich Dad, Poor Dad*—you should make financial decisions with your cold brain and not your emotions. Their eleventh and final point is to have courage. Investing in stocks can be scary, so you need courage to weather the storms.

You should also know what Graham, Lynch and *Forbes* advise not to do. Graham wrote that you should not buy foreign bonds, preferred stocks, secondary common stocks, original offerings and second-grade bonds. For Lynch you should not invest in weak economies but rather in robust ones like America, which he believes still has the best companies and the best system for investing in them. *Forbes* advises against options (puts and calls), warrants, variable hedging, spreading and straddles. All agree that the average investor should avoid margin accounts (those who borrow money from their brokerage company to buy stock).

I believe Graham, Lynch and *Forbes* would also agree on the Eighteenth Rule of How to Get Rich—invest in stocks.

Finally, you should know how to invest in stocks and what vehicle to use. There are smarter, more savvy people in New York who specialize in stocks who know far more than you ever will who lose money all the time. Indeed, Lynch wrote that influential professionals who manage billions of dollars can't agree on whether they are in an economic depression or upswing. How can you possibly beat them? The only way is through time-tested dollar-cost averaging.

Everyone, including Graham, Lynch and *Forbes*, agree that dollar-cost averaging is a wise way to invest in stocks. Graham wrote that the regular purchase of stock since 1949 is certain to be satisfactory since it prevented the practitioner from concentrating his buying at the wrong times, dollar-cost averaging minimizes the risk of paying too much for stocks and the mechanical method of dollar-cost averaging helps avoid crowd psychology. Lynch wrote that the person who ignores the ups and downs of the economy and markets and invests on a regular basis is better off than the person who tries to time his investments. You should dollar-cost average and buy stocks on a regular basis.

So, what is dollar-cost averaging? It is investing similar, specific amounts of cash at regular intervals, perhaps monthly, in stocks over time so the cost becomes less than the average unit price of the stock bought. The secret of the system is that the same dollar amount buys many more low-priced stock units than it does when the market is high. It dampens the effect of buying shares at the top of a bull market.

Acquire stocks through dollar-cost averaging following Graham, Lynch and *Forbes*'s advice. Buy well-established, dividend-paying blue-chip stocks, diversify and hold for a long time; you will not only fulfill the Third Rule of How to Get Rich (save 10 percent of all you earn) but also get rich. Hence, the Nineteenth Rule of How to Get Rich — buy stocks through dollar-cost averaging.

The best vehicle to buy stocks is through an individual retirement account (IRA). There are many forms of IRAs from which you need to choose. IRAs are government-sponsored retirement programs that allow you to invest money, which is sometimes deductible, in investments whose returns are not taxed. This is a great boon and you should take advantage of it to get rich.

The two reasons to invest in an IRA are that they allow for tax-deferred income and compounding. Deferring taxes is important because it allows you to make money now on money you would have paid in taxes, and compounding is important because you are not only getting interest on your initial investment but also interest on interest. This is a deadly combination that will propel you to wealth. I will discuss the different kinds of IRAs and compounding in the next chapter.

You now have some basic information on stocks including how to acquire them and through what vehicle. The next two chapters are about things that enhance and detract from wealth creation.

II

Things that Enhance Wealth Accumulation

Chapter Six

Save, Buy a House, Budget, Own a Business and Carry Insurance

In this chapter, five things will be discussed that enhance wealth creation. The first is to save through a government-sponsored retirement account.

Save

I am assuming you are without a retirement plan other than Social Security (which is a minimal plan), you are not one of those lucky individuals who work for the government with an existing plan or have a corporate pension. Now that you have started saving and buying stocks, you need to set up an individual retirement account (IRA) so your purse begins to fatten. With it, you will begin receiving tax-deferred income, and sometimes you will be able to reduce your income with contributions and benefit from compounding (earning interest on interest).

There are many different plans with different requirements to choose from. Following is a sampling of a few along with some of their general characteristics. Note that you can have more than one plan; this is a good place to seek professional tax advice because of each plan's complexity.

An IRA can be set up individually or by an employer. You can contribute up to $6,000 a year, deduct contributions on your income taxes, buy stocks, make investment decisions yourself or hire a professional, and pay no taxes on investment income and gains until retirement. You are penalized if you withdraw funds before you are fifty-nine-and-a-half years old. A Roth IRA is a little different. You can tribute $5,500 to $6,500 a year, your contributions are made with after-tax dollars, the money generated in the plan is never taxed again, under certain conditions you can withdraw contributions before retirement age and you are not required to take withdraws before age seventy-and-a-half.

The 401(k) plan is a retirement plan for employees that allows contributions up to $19,000 per year in pre-tax income; all income is deferred until it is withdrawn at retirement, and your contributions may be matched by your employer. Finally, the simplified employee pension (SEP) IRA is for self-employed individuals or small business owners; you can contribute up to $56,000 per year or 25 percent of your income, whichever is less, the contributions are deductible and you can withdraw funds any time before age fifty-nine-and-a-half.

These tax-deferred investment vehicles are powerful ways to achieve wealth. To demonstrate this, the savings plan chart below shows how much money a family would have if they followed certain investment guidelines using one of these plans. According to the Census Bureau, the median American household income in 2017 was $61,372 per year. Because this book is about how the average American can become wealthy, let us assume that households with incomes of $40,000, $60,000 and $80,000 per year put 10 percent of their annual income (in monthly installments) in a tax-deferred savings plan that is compounded monthly. Let us also assume that the working career began at age twenty and ended at retirement at sixty-five, a period of forty-five years. Finally, recall that Peter Lynch wrote that over the last seventy years, stocks have gained 11 percent per year. With this in mind, it seems conservative to assume a family could make between 4 percent to 8 percent returns per year in stocks. So, let us assume they obtain returns over forty-five years of 4 percent, 6 percent and 8 percent. The following chart shows how much each household would have at retirement at age sixty-five.

Savings Plan					
(all figures are rounded)					
Investment terms			How much money they would have to retire at age sixty-five		
Annual income	Annual contribution /10 percent of income/ monthly payment	Period	4 percent returns	6 percent returns	8 percent returns
$40,000	$4,000 ($333 per month)	45 years (540 months)	$502,653	$917,745	$1,756,421
$60,000	$6,000 ($500 per month)	45 years (540 months)	$754,734	$1,377,996	$2,637,269
$80,000	$8,000 ($666 per month)	45 years (540 months)	$1,005,306	$1,835,491	$3,512,843

With 8 percent returns, at retirement they would have $1,756,421, $2,637,269 or $3,512,843 — they would be multi-millionaires and rich.

You might rightfully object that it would be difficult to carry on this savings plan for such a long period of time. You could say life has many financial obligations that require money now. The answer is that you are right, but acquiring wealth is difficult, which is why most people never do. Indeed, it is precisely the long period of time that builds your wealth, most of which comes in the later years because you are getting returns on more money. If you waited until your fifties or sixties to start an invest-ment savings account, the amount of wealth you build would be far less than if you start early. Time is your ally, and you must use it to get rich.

This gives the Twentieth Rule of How to Get Rich — in-vest through an IRA — and the Twenty-First Rule of How to Get Rich — start saving in an IRA early.

Buy a House

Arkad's fifth cure for a lean purse was to make thy dwell-ing a profitable investment, so this section is about why buying a house is a profitable investment. Certainly, getting together enough money to purchase a house is difficult for many people. However, there are many imaginative ways to start. There are government low-income programs that help first-time buyers, you could start with a less expensive micro-home or condominium, you could negotiate a con-tract purchase with a very low down payment or you could negotiate a lease with an option to buy, where part of your rental payments apply to the down payment.

The goal is to become a homeowner because of the numerous ways it brings wealth. The first is apprecia-tion, which is just an increase in value due to scarcity and demand. The odds are the house you buy will go up in value. The National Association of Realtors reported that the price of existing homes increased by 5.4 percent annually from 1968 to 2009, so if you bought a home in 1968 for $50,000 and it appreciated at 5.4 percent per year, it would be worth $432,000 in 2009, forty-one years later.

The second reason is leverage, which is the use of a small amount of money to take advantage of a larger asset, which has the potential of amplifying the return on your initial investment. In the case of a house, a simple example would be when you buy house for $100,000 with $10,000 down. If the house appreciates $10,000 in one year, you have made a 100 percent return on your investment or down payment. If it appreciated $20,000, you would have made 200 percent. These are fantastic returns. Be aware, however, that it also works the other way. If, for example, your house declined $10,000 in value, you would have a 100 percent loss and your down payment would be gone.

The third reason is taxes. When you buy a house, some of your interest payments are deductible, which reduces your tax liability. Finally, and most importantly, unlike renting, you end up owning an asset when the loan is paid off. It is a liberating day indeed when you have paid off your mortgage and own your home free and clear.

Once you acquire a house, there are two things you should know that will accelerate your wealth—trading up and prepaying on your mortgage. Using the appreciation example, the house you bought in 1968 for $50,000 would be worth $143,000 twenty years later in 1988 with an approximate 5.4 percent appreciation rate. If you traded your equity into a new house worth about $200,000 in 1998, at the same appreciation rate twenty-one years later, or in 2009, it would be worth about $603,000. By trading up you made $171,000 more due to your trade-up home. Further, there is no tax on some of the gain of your house when you trade up.

The second is to prepay on your mortgage. If you pay a little more on your monthly mortgage, you can dramatically reduce the cost of your house. To use the example of the $200,000 home you traded into, let us assume you have $50,000 in equity and take on a mortgage of $150,000 for twenty years at 5 percent. Your approximate monthly mortgage payment would be about $989. Over twenty years you would end up paying about $237,360 for the house, which includes principle and interest. However, if you prepaid $200 a month in addition to the mortgage, you would be paying about $1,189 a month and you would pay off the mortgage in fifteen years rather than twenty years. With this prepayment, you would end up paying approximately $214,000 for the house and would have saved about $23,360 in payments. What you did was accelerate accumulation of the principle amount, and the result was less interest paid on principle.

One final word of advice: do not move often. Every time you buy or sell a house, there are innumerable fees including real estate commissions, mortgage fees, escrow fees, recording fees and sometimes real estate transfer taxes. You go backward every time you buy a new house, so do it rarely.

So, now you have the evolution of advice on buying a home. Arkad's advice to make thy dwelling profitable became the Eighth Rule of How to Get Rich, which was to buy a house. This leads to the Twenty-Second Rule of How to Get Rich—buy a house and trade up.

Budget

Few people create a budget of their income and expenses, but it is important to do so for many reasons. A budget keeps track of your income and expenses, determines how much money you need to live on, gives a plan on how to spend your money, tells you when you can spend and when not to and helps you live within your means, which helps you avoid debt. In general, a budget gives you an overall view of your financial situation.

Following is a simplified imaginary budget for an average person for illustrative purposes. Its headings are the items you spend money on, what you spent last year, some considerations and what you want to spend next year. It is divided into necessary and unnecessary expenses, which give a snapshot of where you have to spend money and where you do not. It assumes you made $36,360 last year after taxes, which was enough to pay your expenses. It also assumes you want to spend more money, so you need to make $36,660 next year.

Granted, it is difficult for many people to live on $36,360, especially for a family with children, but you still need to know what your income and expenses are. It should be noted that this is an income and expense budget. As you gain wealth, you should also develop a balance sheet that lists your assets, liabilities and net worth.

Budget for an Average Person

Item	Average spent per month last year	Considerations	Monthly expense for next year
NECESSARY ITEMS			
Mortgage or rent	$500	Rent went up 5 percent	$525
Food	$400	Food increased in price about $20 a month	$420
Utilities (electricity, gas, water, garbage, sewer, internet, phone)	$250	Electricity went up $20 a month	$270
Medical (doctor, dentist, prescriptions, health insurance)	$400	Need dental work, increase $10 a month	$410
Auto payment	$200	Will be paid off in mid-year	$100
Insurance (car and home)	$150	No change	$150
Student debt	$250	No change	$250
Other (clothes)	$100	No change	$100
Personal (gas, haircuts, etc.)	$200	No change	$200
Savings	$300	No change	$300
UNNECESSARY ITEMS			
Eating out	$100	No change	$100
Athletic club fee	$80	No change	$80
Travel	$100	Want to travel more	$150
Total	$3,030 per month ($36,360 per year)		$3,055 per month ($36,660 per year)

Last year you spent $36,360, and this year you want to spend $36,660. Although it varies widely for a variety of reasons, let us assume you are paying 15 percent in state, federal and Social Security and Medicare taxes, so before tax you will need to make about $43,000 or about $3,580 per month. If you cannot make that much next year, it becomes clear that you need to either make more money or cut back your expenses. To cut back you could do things like drop the athletic club and jog or keep your travel budget at $100. Conversely, you could increase your income by getting better at your job or find a new higher paying job.

The point is that this budget showed you where you spend your money and how much you need to make, it gave you a plan for future spending and it told you where you have to cut back. Above all, it gave you an overall view of your financial situation, which is a comforting place indeed. Those without a budget are financially blind. This brings the Twenty-Third Rule of How to Get Rich — budget.

Own a Business

One good way to get rich is to own a business. It is not a necessary way but many have achieved wealth by starting a window cleaning business, becoming a self-employed accountant or owning and operating vending machines. The list of business enterprises is endless.

The main advantages of business ownership include that you pay yourself first. Rather than work for another person, you now gain the business income, profits and, if it is a corporation, dividends. You pay yourself and not others. Second, there are tax advantages like deductions for expenses that you can use to reduce your tax liability. Some travel, food, phone bills and car expenses may be deductible. Third, you grow an asset that can become valuable. If you are successful and increase sales, you may end up owning a valuable asset. Finally, there is great satisfaction in being free from an employer and your own boss.

My career was a commercial real estate broker specializing in industrial real estate. When I was young I worked for other commercial real estate companies who took half of my commissions, took much of the credit for the deals I did, constantly evaluated my worth, added an unnecessary layer of office politics to my life and sometimes impeded my ambition to make money. I worked with a frustrating layer of managers above me who cost me money and often decided my fate.

In my early forties I decided I wanted a change and started my own sole proprietorship commercial real estate company that succeeded beyond my wildest dreams. It was a scary time indeed. I had to take on obligations like an office lease, I had to spend money setting up my new enterprise, I had no guaranteed source of income and I could fail and lose everything. But I took a deep breath and worked like a mad man on a mission.

It was one of the best decisions I ever made in life. Gradually I started getting clients and listings and making money. I made more money because there were no managers or in-house cooperating brokers, so most commissions were all mine. I became my own boss; I was working for myself and not another, I made my own decisions, I got more recognition because my name was on the sign and not someone else, I owned a profitable enterprise that paid me money, I got some tax deductions, I felt a sense of freedom, my passion for work was fired up and I felt energized. With my own business I made twice the money with half the stress.

Many people start a business or practice and succeed, but be aware that there are downsides. Most startup businesses fail, so you could lose everything. Further, there is liability, including debt, involved with starting a business that may stay with you if your business fails.

Before you start a business it is important to ask yourself if you're business minded. Do you have the acumen to be a successful business owner? I have a friend who was an excellent craftsman at what he did who tried to turn it into a business and failed. He knew his craft but not pro formas, timing, government issues, billing, salesmanship, accounting, scheduling, taxation, employees, budgeting or management. Owning a business is daunting and requires considerable effort and an organized and knowledgeable business-like mind. It is not for everyone.

Insurance

The final thing that enhances wealth does so by protecting it. Life is full of risks. You could get sick and incur $200,000 in medical bills, get sued for $150,000 for hitting somebody with your car or your house could burn down, causing the loss of a $250,000 asset. These risks take your wealth, and the solution is to carry insurance.

Insurance is a contract with an insurer who promises to pay you a sum of money if specified events occur in the future for a small regular payment known as a premium. The purpose of insurance is to reduce your risk. You should carry it because a catastrophic event and loss could wipe out your hard-earned wealth. You cannot afford to be without it.

The four essential insurance policies are for health, automobile, property and liability. You should get health insurance as soon as possible. It could be through a private insurer or a government program. When you buy a car and start driving, you should carry auto liability and, depending on the value of your car, collision insurance. All states except Virginia and New Hampshire require automobile insurance. You definitely should carry home insurance when you buy a house. In the case of your $250,000 house that burned not, only did you lose an asset and a place to live, but you also may still have a $150,000 mortgage on a nonexistent house! As your wealth increases, you should carry liability insurance. It should be enough to cover your net worth.

There are many other nonessential forms of insurance that you can decide for yourself whether to carry. Some people like life insurance because it provides for loved ones if you die, it can be a savings plan and there are some tax benefits. However, you may be better off using the life insurance premiums to contribute to your IRA and buy common stocks.

Many believe if you start a business or are a professional you should carry errors and omissions insurance. This protects you if you make a business or professional mistake. If you are sloppy or prone to error, you may want to carry it. Many also believe in carrying disability insurance in the event you are unable to work for medical reasons. This is already covered by Social Security that will pay you monthly benefits if you become disabled for many medical reasons before you reach retirement age.

This gives the Twenty-Fourth Rule of How to Get Rich — protect against loss with insurance. So, now let us move on to things that detract from wealth creation.

III

Things that Detract from Wealth Accumulation

Chapter Seven
Inflation, Debt, Taxes and Divorce

Most of this book has been about how to make money and get rich. Some ways included saving, budgeting and setting up an individual retirement account (IRA). This is only half of the equation of wealth acquisition because it is easier to get money than keep it. This chapter will discuss some of the ways wealth dissipates and how to deal with them. Some topics will not be discussed because they are obvious like wasteful spending and gambling, which take wealth.

Inflation

Inflation is a silent devil that imperceptibly robs your wealth. It is the increase in the prices of goods and services over a period of time during which prices rise and currency buys fewer goods and services. It reduces the purchasing power of money. Two causes of inflation are high demand for scarce goods and the government printing excessive currency causing the money supply to outpace economic growth.

In simple terms, inflation lessens your buying power. In chapter six a budget for food next year was set at $420 per month. At a 3.22 percent annual inflation rate compounded over ten years, the same food will cost you about $577 per month. This is a 38 percent increase in your cost of food. Thus, you must increase your income 38 percent just to maintain your standard of living.

Sources disagree on America's rate of inflation. Benjamin Graham wrote that you should assume a 3 percent annual inflation rate, another source states the annual inflation rate over the last twenty years has been 3.22 percent and the consumer price index indicates inflation since the end of World War II, or the last seventy years, has averaged 3.76 percent per year. All scenarios mean that prices in America will double roughly every twenty years. For simplicity and to be conservative, let us assume inflation will continue at an annual rate of 4 percent. What this means to you is you must obtain a return on your investments over 4 percent if you want to get rich.

Beating inflation is a central concern of investors like you. Three strategies involve assets, debt and stocks. James Buchan in his book *Frozen Desire* wrote that the counterpoint of cheap money is expensive property — when the currency in your wallet becomes less valuable, your house becomes more valuable. So, his advice in inflationary times is to get rid of cash and own a valuable asset. When money is cheap you want to own things and buy money, and in deflationary times when money is dear you want to own money and buy things like valuable assets. He added that you should also pay off debts with depreciated currency in inflationary times.

It turns out that companies, and the stocks you own in them, are valuable assets in times of inflation — in most cases the company itself inflates in value. It comes as no surprise then that historically the stock market has outpaced inflation. Indeed, Graham wrote that, unlike bonds, stocks have built-in protection against inflation.

One source stated that for the period from 1950 to 2009, the adjusted return from the stock market has been 7 percent per year. Graham wrote that the Dow Jones averaged an increase of 4 percent per year between 1915 and 1970, so when you add their 4 percent dividend rate, the yield on common stocks has been about 8 percent per year. Always optimistic Peter Lynch wrote that over the last 70 years, stocks have gained 11 percent per year. Whoever is right, the point is in all scenarios stocks beat inflation, hence the emphasis on investing in common stocks in this book in order to become rich.

Debt

In *The Richest Man in Babylon*, George Clason wrote:

> To secure wealth quickly youth often borrows unwisely. Youth, never having had experience, cannot realize that hopeless debt is like a deep pit into which one may descend quickly and where one may struggle vainly for many days. It is a pit of sorrow and regrets where the brightness of the sun is overcast and night is made unhappy by restless sleeping.

In general you should avoid going into debt. Once in debt, it is hard to get out, you get put in a hole, it puts a strain on your finances, it borrows from your future, you can default and face foreclosure or a burdensome deficiency judgment, you may have to declare bankruptcy, which would ruin your credit and it brings, as Clason presaged, sorrow and regret along with stress and often depression.

Further, when you borrow money you usually are required to pay the lender interest. Interest is the cost of using other's money in addition to what you borrowed and is usually expressed as an annual rate. For example, if you paid $30,000 for a car, put $5,000 down and financed the balance over five years at 8 percent, your monthly payment would be about $507 a month. When the debt is eventually paid off, the car would have cost you $35,420 (which includes your down payment) or $5,420 more than the cost of the car. This $5,420 is the interest you paid to use a lender's money.

However, Clason also wrote, "I do not discourage borrowing gold…if it be for a wise purpose." Sometimes debt is a necessary evil you must use wisely in order to get rich. But be aware that there is wise good debt and foolish bad debt.

Good debt is when you buy a necessary asset that appreciates in value, fully amortizes, has good terms and leverage that works for you (amortization is the period of a loan in which debt is paid off with regular payments). Necessary assets include a house, inexpensive car or vocational education. The house will most likely inflate in value, although the car will depreciate in value it is necessary and a vocational education will increase your earning power. Good terms could include a fixed term, low interest rate and no prepayment penalty. Because the house you bought is appreciating in value, you are also obtaining a high return on your down payment, which is leverage working for you. With good debt, you end up with an asset.

Bad debt is when you buy an unnecessary asset that depreciates in value and does not amortize with bad terms, and leverage works against you. Unnecessary sources of bad debt are expensive cars, fancy meals at a restaurant and exotic trips. The expensive car will rapidly depreciate in value, the expensive meal was unnecessary to satiate your hunger and you do not need an exotic trip. Bad terms could include interest-only loans, a high interest rate and a prepayment penalty. Because the expensive car is depreciating in value, you are getting a negative return on your down payment, which is leverage working against you. With bad debt you end up with no assets.

Perhaps the worst bad debt is credit cards. They do not amortize the principle, they have no term and their interest rates are way too high. Some for example charge usurious rates of 15 to 20 percent (usury is unreasonably high interest rates). If you incur credit card debt with a high interest rate and pay only the minimum payment, you are going seriously into more debt. For example, if you owe $5,000 on your credit card at 18 percent per year, you are paying $900 a year or $75 a month in interest. If you pay the minimum monthly amount of $50 you are going further into debt $25 a month, which is $300 more in debt at the end of the year. You are paying money for nothing, which is not the way to get rich.

For many, student loan debt for a four-year college degree is bad debt. One source said the average student loan debt for graduates of four-year colleges in America is $28,650. It is unwise to incur $28,650 in college debt for a job you cannot find that won't pay you enough to pay off the debt. It would be wiser to establish an income and accumulate some savings first and then attend college, paying minimum amounts of tuition over many years out of income to get a baccalaureate degree.

This brings us to the Twenty-Fifth Rule of How to Get Rich — avoid debt.

Taxes

Taxes are a major impediment to getting rich. There are federal taxes like income, Medicare and Social Security, capital gains taxes, business taxes, state taxes, county taxes including real estate taxes, city taxes, tax districts, sales taxes along with a host of hidden taxes like gasoline and tobacco. Depending on your tax situation, you can easily end up paying over half of your income in taxes. To get rich, you need to find ways to reduce your tax burden.

Taxes and how to reduce them is a complex topic that will only be briefly discussed here. There are many legal ways to reduce taxes such as moving out of a high tax rate county, buying high priced items in states with no sales tax and moving your business out of a city that imposes a business tax. One of the most effective ways is to reduce your income. Following are seven ways to do this.

The first very effective way is to contribute money to your IRA. In most cases it reduces your income, reduces your taxes and puts money in your retirement account. The second is to contribute to a qualified charity. A third way is to seek tax-free income such as some gifts or interest on municipal bonds. A fourth way is to take advantage of tax credits such as some expenses for college. The fifth is to take all allowable tax deductions to reduce your income. Some of your real estate taxes are deductible as well as some mortgage interest on your house.

If you operate a business, there are many tax saving deductions that relate to your business that will reduce your taxes. These include vehicle expenses, internet or website fees, costs for professional publications, professional association fees and office supplies. If you work at home, you can also take a home office deduction. Also, you can combine a business trip with a vacation and deduct the cost.

A sixth way is to avoid selling appreciated assets like stock. You would avoid paying any tax on the gain of the asset. There are some more sophisticated ways to reduce your tax liability, one of which is to sell bad investments at a loss to offset a gain somewhere else, which is the seventh way.

The point of all this is in order to get rich you need to keep an eye on your tax liability and do the best to reduce it. This gives the Twenty-Sixth Rule of How to Get Rich — reduce your taxes.

Divorce

The final source of wealth detraction is divorce. This is not a book about marriage, but it is mentioned here briefly because divorce is a significant impediment to getting rich. If you don't think you are marriage material, don't get married, if you do decide to marry, find the right spouse and if you are married with marital problems, get a marriage counselor.

In America about half of all marriages end in divorce. The average marriage lasts about 8.2 years, and only 35 percent of marriages make it to twenty-five years and 6 percent to fifty years. The chances that you will divorce are significant and the financial consequences are devastating. Your wealth will be divided, and you may end up with child support and alimony obligations.

Generally, in community property states, wealth is divided equally while each spouse keeps their separate property. In other states, assets and earnings accumulated during marriage are divided equitably but not necessarily equally. Generally, this means that if you have saved $200,000, you would lose half of it. But this is not all; you could end up with continuing child support and/or alimony payments that will further erode your savings.

Child support varies widely due to many factors. One source said you can pay 12 percent of your gross income for one child, 16 percent for two and 19 percent for three. So, if you make $50,000 a year before taxes, this is $6,000 a year for one child, $8,000 a year for two children and $9,500 for three.

Alimony is a court-ordered allowance for a spouse after divorce. One source said that alimony is sometimes 30 percent of the higher-earning spouse's income minus 20 percent of the lower-earning spouse's. So if you are making $50,000 a year and your ex-spouse $30,000, you could be paying $9,000 per year in alimony. So, if you earn $50,000 a year and are paying child support for two children and alimony based on this formula, you would be paying $17,000 a year and your income would be reduced by 34 percent to $33,000 a year. These are significant impediments to getting rich. Note that these figures are general numbers used for illustrative purposes only. Your obligations may be very different based on many variables. To know how much you would lose and your liability for child support or alimony payments, you should consult a knowledgeable attorney.

Divorce also destroys any family economy of scale. Two adults with children are more economic than two separated adults with children. Two living together sharing expenses is economy of scale because a larger scale lowers average costs. Intact families are efficient because there is one rental or mortgage payment and many services are shared like utility bills, the washing machine and the refrigerator.

Certainly divorce is economically disadvantageous, but it should be mentioned it is also emotionally devastating. It is an emotional upheaval from which some never recover. It involves pain, angst, anger, depression and often damaged children. If you want to marry and get rich, figure out in advance how not to divorce, which is our next topic.

The first thing to do is to honestly evaluate yourself. In chapter one you were asked if you had the character to do what it takes to get rich, now you should ask yourself whether you are suited to marriage. Can you compromise, are you supportive, are you kind and loving, can you support a family and do you think you could be a good parent? If you don't think so then marriage may not be for you.

The second thing to do is honestly evaluate your future spouse. Do they have the characteristics you looked for in yourself? Are they honest, loyal, compatible, frugal, industrious, responsible and stable? Humor and a degree of intelligence also help. You should live with them for a while before you marry in order to learn their true character.

One red flag of a future spouse's suitability to marriage is whether they are from parents who divorced. Judith Wallenstein, Julia Lewis and Sandra Blakeslee in their book *The Unexpected Legacy of Divorce* explained why. Children of intact marriages tend to be good marriage partners because they have been to marriage school. They have watched their parents work out their problems, they are more realistic about marriage, they know what marriage requires and they don't give up a marriage easily. Simply put, they don't expect to divorce.

Children of divorce are different. They watched their parents quit, they do not know the requirements of marriage and they give up easily. They never went to marriage school and may have learned all the wrong lessons. They are more likely to divorce for a number of reasons. Foremost their personality has been made less trusting. They were abandoned once by a parent, so they don't trust others and are quick to abandon others — a kind of "do it to them before they do it to me" mentality. They are more likely to fear commitment and are quick to throw in the towel after an argument and think the marriage is over. They tend to keep their feelings to themselves and have lower expectations. In a way, children from divorce are not grown up.

So if you want to get rich, enter marriage intelligently, which brings us to the Twenty-Seventh Rule of How to Get Rich — don't divorce.

The next chapter will summarize the rules of how to get rich presented throughout this book and the last chapter, under the heading The Big Picture, will offer a few philosophic thoughts on wealth and happiness.

Chapter Eight
The Twenty-Seven Rules
of How to Get Rich

You now have the tools to get rich. You learned Arkad's advice including his rules of gold, how to get a higher paying job, about stocks, things that enhance wealth accumulation including savings plans and things that detract from wealth accumulation. So, go get rich.

The Rules of How to Get Rich are the following:

1. Decide if you have the character to get rich
2. Make the decision to become rich and do what it takes to acquire wealth
3. Save 10 percent of all you earn

4. Control your expenditures through budgeting
5. Spend less than you make
6. Invest and make your gold multiply
7. Carry insurance
8. Buy a house
9. Get a good job and get better at it
10. Listen to the advice of wise men
11. Invest in what you or trusted others know
12. Don't speculate with your savings
13. Be a person of action
14. Never give up
15. Be virtuous
16. Learn salesmanship
17. Learn about stocks
18. Invest in stocks
19. Buy stocks through dollar-cost averaging
20. Invest through an individual retirement account (IRA)
21. Start saving in an IRA early
22. Buy a house and trade up
23. Budget
24. Protect against loss with insurance
25. Avoid debt
26. Reduce your taxes
27. Don't divorce

The last chapter will philosophically discuss a bigger picture, which is the relationship between wealth and happiness.

IV

THE BIG PICTURE

Chapter Nine
Wealth and Happiness

Now that you are rich, you should think about wealth and happiness. Having money is great because it provides financial security and enables you to do the things you want like own a nice home, travel and pursue a hobby. However, in some ways wealth is an empty god that does not bring happiness.

The proverb that money makes a good servant but terrible master is true if you allow money to become your master. Many with money live their lives forever troubled by the responsibilities it brings. They live in constant fear of losing money, unaware that it brings no guarantees. Money also often inflames the passions of envy and anger and sometimes engenders distrust and selfishness. These are not sources of happiness.

Perhaps the most inflammatory emotion money causes is desire. Mentioned earlier, James Buchanan wrote that the world is a battlefield of limitless, unsatisfied wishes, which money makes conspicuous. Some wrongly think that if they can satisfy their limitless desires they will be happy. But many only end up wanting more of what they desire, including more money. They never have enough money, which becomes an empty desired end in itself.

How much money do you really need? In the savings plan chart in chapter six, it was shown that a person making $60,000 a year investing 10 percent of income in common stocks at 6 percent would save $1,377,996 in forty-five years. Invested at 6 percent, this would generate about $82,500 a year or $6,875 a month, which along with your Social Security is more than enough to live comfortably. You don't need more to be happy.

Unrestrained desire only brings unhappiness. Ancient philosophers like Seneca and Boethius believed that endlessly satisfying appetite does not bring happiness. Your life becomes a Ferris wheel going round and round always desiring what you do not have. For these unfortunate souls, the grass is always greener on the other side of the fence only because their desires make them think it is greener. They do not understand if they get there they will still be unhappy because there will be here—they will always be seeking greener pastures.

Indeed, it is ironic to consider that the very nature of money can bring unhappiness. Buchanan wrote that when money enters the system of values it displaces other values—things like love, friendship and ethics are blasted out of existence. Many come to value money over more enduring sources of happiness.

Money often isolates you from other people. Buchanan wrote that money replaces human intercourse and reduces human relationships. When you have money people treat you differently and often artificially. Many with money also lose sight of the natural sources of happiness. It has a way, as Buchanan wrote, to estrange you from the natural world. It becomes more difficult to appreciate the beauty of a sunset or stroll in the woods because your mind is preoccupied with money.

Mentioned earlier, money too often becomes the master. You become dominated by a dead concept rather than actuated by a live feeling. Money becomes your measure of value, so you come to value things in terms of how much they cost and are less likely to value art or a book for their inherent value. Finally, money has a way of speeding up time. It imparts, as Buchanan wrote, a certain urgency to temporal existence, which engenders the view that spending time becomes more important than passing time. Life becomes fast and agitated when you lose the harmony of your natural rhythms.

When you have money, it is important to keep it in perspective. Getting a good night's sleep, enjoying your family and friends and learning and appreciating what you have rather than what money can buy are more enduring sources of happiness. Indeed, Aristotle wrote that happiness consists in a complete life well-lived in accordance with virtue and accompanied by a moderate possession of external goods.

Two life-philosophies that can help you preserve your happiness once you have money are to live simply and be a stoic. Many philosophers have said to be happy simplify your life. Diogenes believed people need little to be happy, Lucretius wrote that nature is easily satisfied and Epicurus taught that life's needs are easy so the happy person should live simply. Cicero believed the happy life depends on little—humans do not need much to be happy. Seneca observed that his poor body is not injured by plain living so one should live simply and in accordance with nature. Epictetus wrote that the man who rids his mind of desire will be untroubled. Marcus Aurelius wrote that if you want to be happy remove superfluity from your life and do little. Russian writer Ivan Turgenev believed that happiness comes when humans perform their natural life functions according to nature because it is conducive to a quiet happy life.

English philosopher Bertrand Russell echoed Turgenev's sentiments when he wrote that the rhythm of life is slow, nature is slow and the happy life is the quiet life. American philosopher and naturalist Henry David Thoreau summarized these philosophers' views with the simple admonition to *simplify, simplify, simplify*. Simplicity brings a contented and happy life because you are satisfying your simple instinctual desires. Finally, contemporary writer M. M. Kirsch in his book *How to Get Off the Fast Track and Live a Life Money Can't Buy* wrote that happiness and fulfillment come from living a life of simplicity that allows the individual time to wonder and appreciate the simple joys in life. To live the good life is to be able to control one's life and one's destiny and not be at the mercy of the marketplace. So, live simply and avoid wanting more.

Stoicism is an ancient philosophy whose goal was to bring human happiness. Three of its principle tenets that intended to bring happiness were that the world is as you make it and that you should avoid passion and remain indifferent to that which you cannot control.

Reality bombards you daily with impressions that affect how you feel. You have no control over what bombards you, but you do have control over what you think about it. You can choose to view an impression good or bad and thus control how you feel about it. Happiness to the stoics, then, is a choice, and people have the ability to make the choices that make their lives happy. Epictetus wrote that one choice is to adjust our desires to the way the world is rather than trying to adjust the world to satisfy our desires. Hence, the first tenet is that the world is as you make it, so adopt the beliefs that make it a place that makes you happy.

Their second tenet is to avoid emotions and especially passion. From this tenet the word stoic wrongfully has come to denote a person with no emotion or one who is in iron control of their passions. In truth, the stoics advocated avoiding the passions that lead to unhappiness such as anger, envy, hate and fear. With anger, for example, you burn for revenge, which only makes you angrier and unhappy. Hence, the second tenet means is to avoid negative passions.

Their third tenant deals with fate and fortune. Their view is that there are some things that will happen to you like dying that you have no control over, so they ask: why worry about it? Fate tells us we will die and fortune determines how. For the stoics, it is useless to fret and worry over matters beyond your control, hence the third tenet, which is to remain indifferent to that which is beyond our control.

Epictetus once wrote that you should be happy because God made you that way. He also wrote that you are responsible for your own happiness because ultimately it comes from within. So to make yourself happy, you must make money your slave and not your master. Money can help you achieve happiness, but it is not necessary.

Always keep in mind that your life is more than money. You should live your life to the fullest now. Jean-Jacques Rousseau in *Emile* wrote that most people only worry about tomorrow and fail to live today enjoying the moment and Sophocles that it is a mistake to wait till the evening to see how splendid the day has been. Have fun, enjoy the sweetness of life and do not give into rushing for money. The goal of life is not the grave or to be the richest man in the cemetery but rather to enjoy the journey.

About the Author

John L. Bowman lives in Portland, Oregon, where he raised three daughters with his wife Kathy. He is the author of numerous books on philosophy, real estate, politics, sports, words, stoicism and humor. He received a Bachelor of Arts degree in 1973 from Whitman College, a Bachelor of Arts degree in philosophy in 1993 from Portland State University and a Master of Interdisciplinary Studies degree in philosophy and history in 2010 from Oregon State University. Much of his knowledge regarding wealth came from his forty years in business as a commercial real estate broker specializing in industrial properties. He owned and operated his own commercial real estate practice John L. Bowman, Real Estate for over twenty years.

His books and biography can be viewed on his website at johnlbowman.com. You can send him an email directly at author@johnlbowman.com. Readers can also view his Amazon author page at https://www.amazon.com/-/e/B001K6KNDW.

Thanks for reading my book. I hope it makes you rich.
— John Bowman

Books by John L. Bowman

Reflections on Man and the Human Condition
Selected Topics in Philosophy
Nobody's Perfect
How to Succeed in Commercial Real Estate
Socialism in America
God's Lecture
A Reader's Companion
Stoicism, Enkrasia and Happiness
Aegean Summer
The Art of Volleyball Hitting
Graduate School
Provocative and Contemplative Quotations
On Law
A Reference Guide to Stoicism
A Reader's Companion II
Democracy and Why It Will Fail in America
Philosophy and Happiness
My Travels (unpublished)
How to Get Rich
A Reader's Companion III (in production)